100 FACTS
Ancient Greece

100 FACTS
Ancient Greece

Fiona Macdonald

Consultant: Rupert Matthews

Sandy Creek
NEW YORK

An Imprint of Sterling Publishing
387 Park Avenue South
New York, NY 10016

Publishing Director: Belinda Gallagher
Creative Director: Jo Cowan
Assistant Editor: Sarah Parkin
Editorial Assistant: Claire Philip
Volume Designer: Joe Jones
Image Manager: Lorraine King
Indexer: Jane Parker
Production Manager: Elizabeth Collins
Reprographics: Anthony Cambray, Stephan Davis
Archive Manager: Jennifer Hunt
Assets: Lorraine King

ISBN 978-1-4351-5082-9

ACKNOWLEDGMENTS
The publishers would like to thank the following artists
who have contributed to this book:
Mike Foster, Richard Hook, Colin Livingstone, Patricia Ludlow,
Andrea Morandi, Mike Saunders, Mike White
Cover artwork: Mike White
All other artworks from the Miles Kelly Artwork Bank

The publishers would like to thank the following sources for the use of their photographs:
Back cover: Federico Rostagno/Shutterstock.com; Page 14 2004 Credit: Topham Picturepoint TopFoto.co.uk;
17 Charles Stirling (Diving)/Alamy; 22–23 TopFoto TopFoto.co.uk; 27(t) The Art Archive/Corbis,
(bl) Patrick Frilet/Rex Features; 39 Richard Cummins/Corbis; 41 KPA/Zuma/Rex Features;
42–43 Jose Fuste Raga/Corbis; 47(br) Aliki Sapountzi/Aliki Image Library/Alamy

All other photographs are from:
Corel, digitalSTOCK, digitalvision, iStockphoto.com, John Foxx, PhotoAlto,
PhotoDisc, PhotoEssentials, PhotoPro, Stockbyte

Every effort has been made to acknowledge the source and copyright holder of each picture.
Miles Kelly Publishing apologizes for any unintentional errors or omissions.

Made with paper from a sustainable forest

Manufactured in China
Lot #:
2 4 6 8 10 9 7 5 3 1

05/13

Contents

Greece was great

1 **Ancient Greece was a small country, but its people had great ideas.** From around 2000 B.C., they created a splendid civilization that reached its peak between 500–400 B.C. All citizens contributed to a society that respected people's rights, encouraged the best in human nature and lived in harmony with the natural world. Today, we still admire Greek sport, medicine, drama, politics, poetry, and art.

▲ The agora (town square) of Athens was a meeting place for citizens and an open-air market. Traders sold fresh fruit and vegetables and craftworkers sold cloth and pottery.

Greek homelands

2 **The Greeks thought that they were better than other people.** They saw all foreigners as uncivilized "barbarians" who did not share the same values and beliefs, or follow the Greeks' lifestyle. Even worse, they did not speak or understand the elegant Greek language.

3 **Lifestyle was shaped by the seasons.** Winters were cold with icy winds, pouring rain, and storms. Summers were very hot and dry with droughts, dust, and forest fires. Spring was green and fresh—a time to plant crops and fight wars. Fall, with its harvest of ripe olives, grapes, and grain, was the busiest time for farmers.

▼ Neat rows of olive trees growing on a Greek farm. Olives were mixed with salt then stored in jars to eat, or crushed to make oil.

▼ The Greeks' homeland included mainland Greece and over 2,000 islands in the Aegean Sea and the Ionian Sea, together with the coast of Asia Minor.

THRAC

MACEDONIA

Mount Olympus

GREECE

IONIAN SEA

Olympia

Athens

Sparta

Troy

ASIA MINOR

GEAN SEA

Ephesus

THERA

CRETE

▲ The land of Greece was rugged and mountainous. Today, the stony soil is bare. In ancient Greek times there would have been more trees.

4 **Ancient Greece was bigger than Greece is today.** The power and influence of Greek civilization traveled far beyond mainland Greece and the nearby islands. Greek people, ideas, designs, and language could be found along the Mediterranean and the Black Sea coasts.

5 **Sited in an active earthquake zone, Greece was regularly hit by tremors.** Some quakes were minor, but others were more serious. They knocked down houses, started fires and landslides, wrecked water supplies, and blocked important harbors. Earthquakes killed and injured many citizens.

I DON'T BELIEVE IT!

Around 1450 B.C., a Greek island disappeared! Most of Thera vanished when a volcano erupted there. The explosion triggered earthquakes, tsunamis, and dust clouds that damaged many other Greek islands.

Steeped in history

6 The ancient Greeks were proud of their beautiful country. There were high snowy mountains, swift rushing streams, thick forests, flowery meadows, and narrow, fertile plains beside the sea. Around the coast there were thousands of rocky islands, some small and poor, others large and prosperous.

◄ A carved stone figure of a woman found in the Cyclades Islands. The design is very simple but strong and graceful.

▼ This timeline shows some of the important events in the history of ancient Greece.

7 Greek civilization began on the islands. Some of the first evidence of farming in Greece comes from the Cyclades Islands. Around 6000 B.C., people living there began to plant grain and build villages. They buried their dead in graves filled with treasures, such as carved marble figures, pottery painted with magic sun symbols, and gold and silver jewelry.

TIMELINE OF GREECE

c. 40,000 B.C.
First people in Greece. They are hunters and gatherers

c. 2000–1450 B.C.
Minoan civilization on the island of Crete

c. 1250 B.C.
Traditional date of the Trojan War

c. 900–700 B.C.
Greek civilization grows strong again

c. 6000 B.C.
First farmers in Greece

c. 1600–1100 B.C.
Mycenean civilization on mainland Greece

c. 1100–900 B.C.
A time of decline—kingdoms weaken, writing stops

c. 776 B.C.
Traditional date of first Olympic Games

◀ This jar, made around 900 B.C., is rather dull and plain. It suggests that times were troubled and Greek people had no money to spare for art.

8 **Between 1100–900 B.C., the history of Greece is a mystery.** From 2000–1100 B.C., powerful kings ruled Greece. They left splendid buildings and objects behind them, and used writing. But between around 1100–900 B.C., there were no strong kingdoms, little art, few new buildings—and writing disappeared.

▲ Alexander the Great conquered an empire stretching from Greece to India.

9 **Migrants settled in distant lands.** By around 700 B.C., Greece was overcrowded. There were too many people, not enough farmland to grow food and some islands were short of water. Greek families left to set up colonies far away, from southern France to North Africa, Turkey, and Bulgaria.

10 **When the neighbors invaded, Greek power collapsed.** After 431 B.C., Greek cities were at war and the fighting weakened them. In 338 B.C., Philip II of Macedonia (a kingdom north of Greece) invaded with a large army. After Philip died, his son, Alexander the Great, made Greece part of his mighty empire.

c. 700–500 B.C.
Greeks set up colonies around Mediterranean Sea

c. 480–479 B.C.
Greece fights invaders from Persia (now Iran)

c. 338 B.C.
Philip II of Macedonia conquers Greece

c. 147–146 B.C.
Romans conquer Greece and Macedonia

c. 500–430 B.C.
Athens leads Greece, creates amazing art, has democratic government

c. 431–404 B.C.
Wars between Athens and Sparta

c. 336–323 B.C.
Alexander the Great of Macedonia and Greece conquers a vast empire

Kings and warriors

11 **King Minos ruled an amazing palace city.** The first great Greek civilization grew up at Knossos on the island of Crete. Historians call it "Minoan" after its legendary king, Minos. Around 2000 B.C., Minoan kings built an amazing palace-city, with rooms for 10,000 people. It was decorated with wonderful frescoes (wall paintings), statues and pottery.

▲ A section of the palace at Knossos on the island of Crete. A succession of powerful kings ruled a rich kingdom here.

12 **Minoan Greeks honored a monster.** Greek myths describe how a fearsome monster was kept in a labyrinth (underground maze) below the palace. It was called the Minotaur, and it was half-man, half-bull.

▲ Greek legends told how the young hero Theseus bravely entered the labyrinth and killed the Minotaur.

QUIZ

1. What was the Minotaur?
2. What was the labyrinth?
3. Where was Knossos?

Answers:
1. A monster—half-man, half-bull 2. A maze underneath the Minoan royal palace 3. On the Greek island of Crete

► This golden mask was found in one of the royal tombs at Mycenae. It covered the face of a king who died around 1500 B.C.

Oule = Hello

Khaire = Goodbye

13 **Invaders brought the Greek language.** Between around 2100–1700 B.C., warriors from the north arrived in mainland Greece. They brought new words with them and their language was copied by everyone else living in Greece.

▼ Works of art found at Knossos include many images of huge, fierce bulls with athletes leaping between their horns in a deadly religious ritual.

14 **Mycenae was ruled by warrior kings.** Around 1600 B.C. new kings took control of Minoan lands from forts on the Greek mainland. The greatest fort was at Mycenae, in the far south of Greece. Mycenaean kings sent traders to Egypt and the Near East to exchange Greek pottery and olive oil for gold, tin, and amber. They used their wealth to pay for huge tombs in which they were buried.

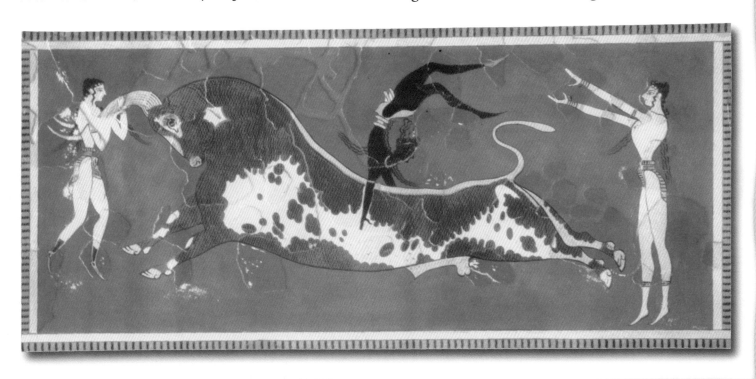

War with Troy

15 A famous Greek poem, the Iliad, describes a terrible war between the Greeks and the Trojans. The Trojans lived in a rich city on the west coast of Asia Minor (now Turkey). The Iliad was first written down around 750 B.C. Ancient Greeks said the writer was a blind poet called Homer.

▼ A scene from the 2004 film *Troy*, starring Brad Pitt. The war between the Trojans and the Greeks still thrills people today. Some of the story is legend, but it may be based on real, half-remembered, facts.

MAKE HELEN'S CROWN

You will need:
gold-colored card   ruler   scissors
sticky tape   glue   gold plastic
"jewels" or sequins   strings of beads

1. Cut a strip of gold-colored card about 6 in wide and 26 in long.
2. Tape the ends of the strip together, to make a circular "crown."
3. Decorate your crown with "jewels" or sequins.
4. Add strings of beads hanging down at the back and the sides.

16 Queen Helen loved a Trojan prince. According to legend, the Trojan War started because Helen, the wife of Greek King Menelaus, ran away with (or was captured by) Paris, a Trojan prince. However, historians believe the main reason for the war was because the Greeks and the Trojans were rival traders.

17 **The Greeks could not break through Troy's walls until they thought of a clever plan.** They made a huge, hollow, wooden horse, hid warriors inside and persuaded the Trojans to accept it as an offering to the gods. The Trojans hauled the horse into their city, then the Greeks leaped out and defeated them.

18 **Odysseus survived to have amazing adventures.** Another famous Greek poem tells how the warrior Odysseus fought at Troy, then on the way home survived extraordinary encounters with gods, giants, witches, one-eyed monsters, sea-serpents, and a man-eating whirlpool.

▶ The Cyclops was a one-eyed giant. He trapped Odysseus and his soldiers in a cave and planned to eat them. But Odysseus blinded the Cyclops, escaped from the cave and sailed away.

▶ The *Iliad* describes how, for ten years, the Greeks besieged the city of Troy. They eventually won the war by offering a wooden horse to the Trojans. Once inside the city walls, warriors leapt out of the horse and destroyed the city.

City-states

19 The power of Mycenaean kings collapsed around 1200 B.C. By 700 B.C., Greece had been divided into 300 city-states, which were cities and the land around them. Some city-states were ruled by kings, some by tyrants (men who governed by force) and some by oligarchs (small groups of rich, powerful men).

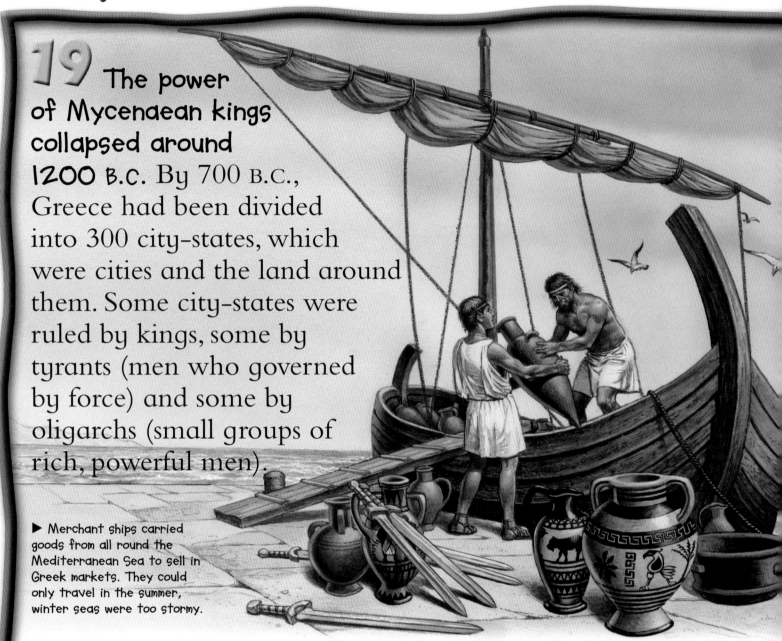

▶ Merchant ships carried goods from all round the Mediterranean Sea to sell in Greek markets. They could only travel in the summer, winter seas were too stormy.

20 Most city-states grew rich by buying and selling. The agora (market place) was the center of many cities. Goods on sale included farm produce such as grain, wine and olive oil, salt from the sea, pottery, woolen blankets, sheepskin cloaks, leather sandals, and slaves.

21 Top craftsmen made fine goods for sale. Cities were home to many expert craftsmen. They ran small workshops next to their homes, or worked as slaves in factories owned by rich businessmen. Greek craftworkers were famous for producing fine pottery, stone carvings, weapons, armor, and jewelry.

22 **Coins displayed city wealth and pride.** They were invented in the Near East around 600 B.C. Their use soon spread to Greece, and each city-state issued its own designs, stamped out of real silver. Coins were often decorated with images of gods and goddesses, heroes, monsters, and favorite local animals.

▶ The design on the top coin shows the head of Alexander the Great. The other is decorated with an owl, the symbol of Athens' guardian goddess, Athena.

◀▲ The walls and gates guarding the city of Mycenae were made of huge stone slabs. The gate had a huge sculpture of two lions above it.

23 **Cities were defended by strong stone walls.** City-states were proud, independent, and quarrelsome. They were often at war with their rivals. They were also in constant danger of attack from neighboring nations, especially Persia (now Iran). To protect their homes, temples, workshops, market places, and harbors, citizens built strong wooden gates and high stone walls.

▶ Many Greek ships were wrecked together with their cargoes. Some have survived on the seabed for over 2,000 years and are studied by divers today.

QUIZ

1. What was a city-state?
2. What was the center of many cities?
3. What were coins made of?
4. How did the Greeks defend their cities?

Answers:
1. A city and the land around it
2. The agora (market place) 3. Real silver 4. With strong wooden gates and high stone walls

Citizens, foreigners, slaves

► Slaves for sale. Men, women, and children captured in war or snatched by pirates were put on display for rich families to buy.

24 Within most city-states, there were different classes of people. Citizens were men who had been born in the city-state, together with their wives and children. Foreigners were traders, sailors, or traveling artists and scholars. Slaves belonged to their owners.

25 In wealthy city-states almost half the population were slaves. Household slaves did the shopping, cooking, housework, and child care. Gangs of slave-laborers worked for rich citizens or city governments as builders, road-menders, miners, and security guards. Slaves could be very badly treated. The conditions for slaves working in mines and on building sites were grim and many died.

26 In 508 B.C., Athenian leader Cleisthenes established a new system of government called "democracy" (rule by the people). All male citizens over 18 years old could speak and vote at city Assemblies, elect the officials that ran their city-state and be elected as city councillors. Women, foreigners, children, and slaves had no democratic rights.

27 In Athens, citizens could make speeches at the Assembly to propose new laws for their community. They served as jurors in the city-state law courts, hearing the evidence against accused criminals and deciding whether they were innocent or guilty. Citizens could also take part in debates on important government decisions, such as whether to declare war.

▼ Speeches at the Athenian Assembly were carefully timed (and kept short) so that all citizens would have a chance to share in the debate.

▼ You can see the names of two unpopular Athenian citizens scratched on these pieces of pottery. Left, top line: Themistokles. Right, top line: Kimon.

28 Once a year, Athenian citizens voted to ban unpopular people from their city for ten years. They scratched the name of the person they wanted to remove on an ostrakon (piece of broken pottery). If 6,000 citizens (about a quarter of the whole Assembly) voted to ban the same man, he had to leave the city within ten days.

Mighty Athens

29 **Athens was the greatest city in Greece.** Between 510–431 B.C., it was the leading Greek city-state. Athens owned some of the best farmland, a port with a fine harbor, fabulous silver mines, and a well-trained citizen army. All these made it rich, strong and confident.

▶ A steep winding road leads up to the Parthenon temple from the city far below. On festival days, processions of citizens lead prize animals along it to sacrifice to the goddess Athena.

30 **The Acropolis ("high city") was a holy hill and ancient fortress that overlooked Athens.** Many fine buildings stood there, including the magnificent Parthenon temple. Built between 447 B.C. and 432 B.C., it housed a 50-foot-high gold-and-marble statue of Athena, the city's guardian goddess.

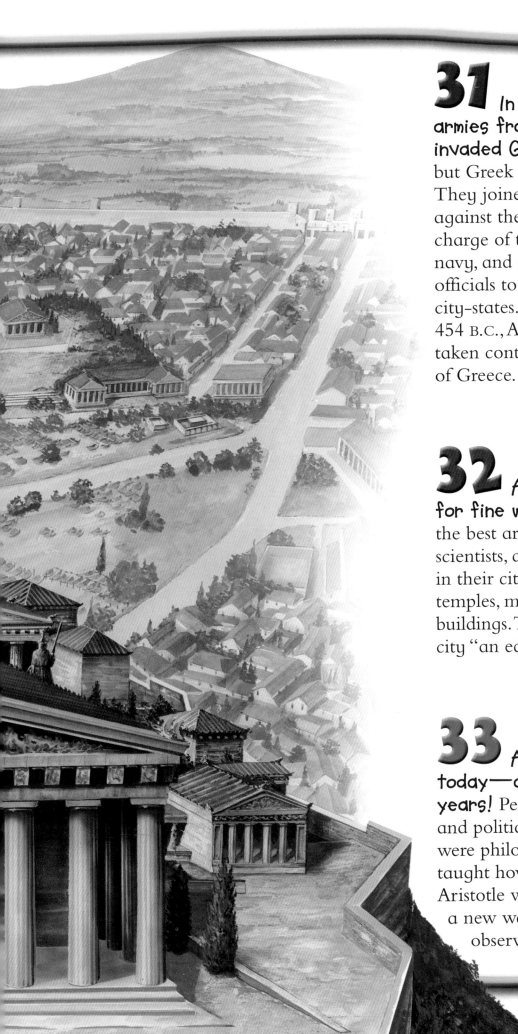

31 In 490 and 480 B.C., armies from Persia (now Iran) invaded Greece. They were defeated, but Greek city-states felt threatened. They joined together in a League against the Persians. Athens took charge of the League, built a splendid navy, and sent soldiers and government officials to "advise" other city-states. By around 454 B.C., Athens had taken control of most of Greece.

32 Athenian city leaders paid for fine works of art. They invited the best artists, architects, sculptors, scientists, and scholars to live and work in their city, and gave money to build temples, monuments, and public buildings. They vowed to make their city "an education to Greece."

33 Athenians are famous today—after more than 2,000 years! Pericles was a great general and political leader. Socrates and Plato were philosophers and teachers who taught how to think and question. Aristotle was a scientist who pioneered a new way of studying by carefully observing and recording evidence.

Sparta

34 **Sparta was Athens' great rival.** It was a city-state set in wild mountain country in the far south of Greece. Sparta had kings who ruled together with a small elite group of citizens. Other Spartans were either free craftsmen who were not allowed to vote, or helots who had few rights but made up 80 percent of the population.

35 **Sparta was always ready for war.** Kings and citizens lived in fear that the helots might rebel. So all male Spartans had to train as warriors. After this, they were sent to live in barracks with other soldiers, ready to fight at any time.

36 **All Spartan citizens were warriors.** Soldiers were famous for their bravery and loyalty—and for their bright red cloaks and long curling hair. Their main duty was to fight. They had no time to grow food, keep farm animals, build houses, make clothes, or buy and sell. All these tasks, and more, were done by helot families.

I DON'T BELIEVE IT!

When their sons were marching off to war Spartan women said "Come back carrying your shield (victorious) or carried on it (dead!)."

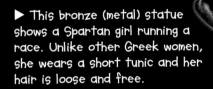

▶ This bronze (metal) statue shows a Spartan girl running a race. Unlike other Greek women, she wears a short tunic and her hair is loose and free.

38 **Women in Sparta were strong, like men.** Young girls were made to do tough physical training. The Spartans believed this would make them grow up to produce strong, warlike sons. The girls were educated in reading and writing to the same level as the boys. Spartan women had to be emotionally tough as they spent most of their lives apart from their husbands and had to give up their children to serve the city-state.

37 **Spartan children were trained to be tough.** Citizen children were sent to state training camps. There, boys were treated very harshly so that they would learn to be tough and not complain. From seven years old they were taught to fight, kept cold and hungry, and beaten so that they would learn to endure pain.

◀ The legendary toughness of Spartan warriors has inspired artists and film-makers. This scene, from the film 300, shows the Spartans' metal helmets, sharp spears, and round shields.

War on land and sea

39 As teenagers, all Greek male citizens were trained to fight. They had to be ready to defend their city whenever danger threatened. City-states also employed men as bodyguards and mercenary troops with special skills.

▼▶ Soldiers had different duties. Cavalrymen were messengers and spies. Peltasts had to move fast and were armed with javelins. Mercenaries fought for anyone who would pay them.

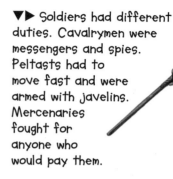

Peltast

Hoplite

Cavalry

Mercenary

40 Each soldier paid for his own weapons and armor. Most soldiers were hoplites (soldiers who fought on foot). Their most important weapons were swords and spears. Poor men could not afford swords or armor. Their only weapons were slings for shooting stones and simple wooden spears.

41 Soldiers rarely fought on horseback. At the start of a battle, hoplites lined up side by side with their shields overlapping, like a wall. Then they marched toward the enemy while the peltasts threw their javelins. When they were close enough, the hoplites used their spears to fight the enemy.

◀ A Corinthian-style helmet. Soldiers tried to protect themselves from injury with bronze helmets, breastplates, greaves (shin guards), and round wooden shields.

Ancient Greek soldiers rarely rode horses—because stirrups had not yet been invented. Without stirrups to support him, a soldier on horseback who hurled a spear or stabbed with a sword was likely to fall off backward!

▼ Greek ships were made of wood. If they were holed below the waterline they sank very quickly.

42 City-states paid for fleets of fast, fearsome wooden warships, called triremes. Each ship had a crew of about 170 oarsmen who sat in three sets of seats, one above the other. They rowed the ship as fast as they could toward enemy vessels, hoping that the sharp, pointed ram at its prow would smash or sink them. The most famous naval battle in Greece was fought at Salamis, near Athens, in 480 B.C., when the Greeks defeated the Persians.

Farming and fishing

43 **Cities were surrounded by fields and farms.** Everyone living inside the walls relied on country people to grow crops, raise animals, and bring food to sell at city markets. Some rich families owned country farms as well as city houses and workshops. They paid for servants or slaves to work the land for them.

▲ Satyrs (legendary monsters) picking and crushing ripe grapes to extract the juice to make wine.

44 **Farmers worked hard to make a living.** The climate was harsh and they had no big machines to help them. Men plowed the soil, cut down trees, sheared sheep, and harvested grain. Women milked sheep and goats, made cheese, grew vegetables, kept chickens and bees, and gathered wild herbs and berries. Children scared birds from crops and watched over sheep and goats.

45 **Grain, grapes, and olives were the most valuable crops.** Barley was the chief grain crop. It was used to make porridge or flour. Grapes were dried in the sun, or trampled by bare feet to extract the juice. This was turned into wine. Olives were crushed to produce oil. This was used in cooking, for burning in lamps, or for cleaning and smoothing the skin.

▼ Sheep's wool was cleaned, combed, spun into thread then woven to make warm clothes, rugs, and blankets.

46 The Greeks hunted in wild countryside. Mountains and steep valleys were covered in thick forests. Wild creatures lived there, such as wolves, bears, boar, and deer. Huntsmen tracked and killed them for their skins or meat. They also trapped wild birds and stole eggs from their nests, and caught small creatures to eat such as hares and rabbits.

▲ A wild boar hunt (top) pictured on a Greek pot made around 600 B.C.

47 Coastal communities made a living from fishing. Every day fishermen sailed out to catch tuna, mullet, squid, octopus, and many other sea creatures. Villagers worked as boat-builders and sail-makers, or made ropes and fishing nets. Women prepared bait and preserved fish by drying or smoking to eat in winter.

▶ This wall painting from Minoan Crete shows a fisherman carrying home his catch of gleaming fresh fish.

48 Divers searched for sea produce to sell. They plunged deep underwater, holding their breath for as long as they could. They searched for shellfish (to eat and use as dye for cloth) and sponges, which the Greeks used when bathing. Sponges were also useful for doctors—they soaked up blood.

▼ A modern display of Greek seafood. Fish and shellfish might have been even better in ancient Greek times because the Mediterranean Sea was less polluted.

Food and drink

49 **Greek food was plain, hearty, and healthy.** It included whole grains, cheese, beans and lentils, fruits, vegetables, olives, and for special occasions— a little meat or fish.

▶ Preparing a meal in an open-air kitchen in the courtyard of a house. Food was cooked over a wood fire in a stone hearth.

Mixing barley and honey to make cakes

Oil and wine stored in jars

Slabs of stone or pottery tiles for floor

All the cooking was done by hand

Stone hearth with metal racks for cooking

50 **Main meals were breakfast and dinner.** Breakfast was bread dipped in olive oil or stale wine. Dinner was olives, then eggs, dried bean stew, or hot barley porridge. This was followed by vegetables, fruit, and honeycomb. Some people ate a light lunch of bread with fruit or cheese.

▼ A pottery bowl decorated with tasty-looking fish.

51 **Greek cooking was very simple.** Boiling, stewing, or grilling were the only methods of cooking. Many foods were eaten raw, such as fruit, herbs, and some shellfish. The Greeks disapproved of cooked dishes with lots of different ingredients, saying that they were too indulgent.

Cooking pots stored on wooden shelf

Walls of rough plaster

Table of scrubbed wood

52 The Greeks enjoyed wine —but always mixed it with water. Wine could be rough, strong, and unsuitable for drinking. People also thought that drunkenness was shameful, except at parties for men only. They did not want to see their guests disgracing themselves.

53 There might be hungry months in winter. Meals were based on preserved foods and grain from the summer harvest. If these ran out or decayed, families went hungry. The only food preservation techniques were smoking, pickling, steeping in olive oil, or drying in the sun.

54 Dinner parties were for men only. When husbands invited their male friends to a symposion (dinner party), their wives and daughters stayed away. At a party, male diners reclined on couches while slaves served food and wine.

▶ Male guests at a symposion relax while listening to a girl—probably a slave—playing the double flute.

Family life

55 **Families were very important.** A person's wealth, rank, and occupation all depended on their family circumstances, as did the part they played in community life. Some families were very active in politics and had powerful friends—and enemies.

56 **Fathers were the heads of families.** They had power over everyone in their households—wives, children, and slaves. However, families also worked as a team to find food, make a safe, comfortable home, and train their children in all the skills they would need in adult life.

Bedrooms were upstairs

Pottery tiles

Mud brick walls covered with plaster

Slaves cooked in the kitchen

Prayers were said around the altar each morning

57 **All Greek parents longed for a son.** Boys passed on the family name to the next generation and they could protect family property and run businesses or farms. However, girls had to be fed and housed at the family's expense, then they left to get married.

▲ Greek houses were designed to provide security and privacy. They had high, windowless outer walls and a hidden inner courtyard, which only the inhabitants and trusted visitors could see.

58 Most girls married very young, aged around 13 years. Their husbands, who were several years older, were chosen by their fathers for political or business reasons. A marriage linked two familes together. Romantic love was not important in marriage —the Greeks thought it was dangerous!

▼ Weddings took place at dusk. The bride was driven to the bridegroom's family home, accompanied by guests carrying flaming wooden torches.

59 Women did not have the same rights as men. Many women had strong opinions about city and community life. A few were also well-educated and interested in the latest ideas. However, according to the law, women could not vote, make a public speech, or take any part in politics.

60 Funerals were important family occasions. Wives and daughters spent most of their lives at home. However, they were allowed to attend family funerals. All family members said prayers together and made offerings to the gods in memory of the dead person.

Education

61 From their earliest days, children were expected to play their part in the family. This meant being well-behaved, obedient, sharing family worship of the gods, and showing respect to their parents.

QUIZ
1. At what age did boys start school?
2. Name three subjects boys studied there.
3. Name two favorite Greek sports.

Answers:
1. Around seven years old
2. Reading, writing, arithmetic, how to sing or play a musical instrument, how to debate and recite poetry 3. Running, jumping, wrestling, throwing the javelin

▲ A schoolroom scene, pictured on a Greek pot, showing a music lesson, a writing lesson, and a slave. The slave is there to make sure that his master's son behaves and works hard.

62 From around seven years old, boys from wealthy families went to school. They learned reading, writing, simple arithmetic, how to sing or play a musical instrument, and how to debate and recite poetry. They also practiced favorite Greek sports such as running, jumping, wrestling, and throwing the javelin.

63

School was not for girls.
They stayed at home and learned skills such as spinning, weaving, and cookery. Wealthy women taught their daughters how to read and write, keep accounts, manage a big household, and give orders. Older women also passed on traditional songs and dances so that girls could take part in religious festivals.

▲ This statue shows a slave girl mixing flour, yeast, and water to make bread.

65

Socrates was a scholar and teacher who lived in Athens.
He encouraged his students to try to discover the truth by asking careful, thoughtful questions. However, his constant questioning alarmed political leaders who accused him of misleading young people. Socrates was condemned to death by the Athens law courts and given poison. He died in 399 B.C.

64

Most boys left school when they were 14 years old.
Older boys might study with local scholars or sophists (traveling teachers). Around 380 B.C., a man called Plato opened a study center in Athens called the Academy. He planned to train young men to work for the city-state, but attracted the best students in Greece who became famous for their brilliant ideas.

▶ Plato believed that thinking and learning were essential for a good life.

Clothes and fashion

66 Greek clothes were just draped around the body. They were loose and flowing, for comfort in the hot summer months. For extra warmth in winter, both men and women draped a thick wooly himation (cloak) over their shoulders.

▶ Men's clothing was designed for action. Young men wore short tunics so they could work—and fight—easily. Older men's robes were longer.

67 Each piece of cloth used to make a garment was specially made. It had to be the right length and width to fit the wearer. All cloth was handwoven, usually by women in their homes. Cool, smooth linen was the favorite cloth for summer. In winter, Greeks preferred cozy wool. Very rich people wore fine clothes of silk imported from India.

◀ Women's clothing was modest and draped the body from top to toe. Respectable women covered their heads and faces with a veil when they went outside the house.

MAKE A GREEK CHITON

You will need:
Length of cloth twice as wide as your outstretched arms and half your height
safety pins   belt or length of cord

1. Fold the cloth in half.

2. Fasten two edges of the cloth together with safety pins. In the middle, leave a gap of about 12 in.

3. Pull the cloth over your head so that the safety pins sit on your shoulders.

4. Fasten the belt or cord around your waist. Pull some of the cloth over the belt so that the cloth is level with your knees.

68
Women—and men—took care of their skin. To keep their skin smooth and supple, men and women rubbed themselves all over with olive oil. Rich women also used sunshades or face powder to achieve a fashionably pale complexion. They did not want to look suntanned—that was for farm workers, slaves—and men!

Before 500 B.C.

500–300 B.C.

After 300 B.C.

69
Curls were very fashionable. Women grew their hair long and tied it up with ribbons or headbands, leaving long curls trailing over their shoulders. Men, except for Spartan warriors, had short curly hair. Male and female slaves had their hair cropped very short—this was a shameful sign.

▲ Before 500 B.C., long, natural hairstyles were popular. Between 500–300 B.C., women tied their hair up and held it in place with ribbons or scarves. After 300 B.C., curled styles and jeweled hair ornaments were popular and men shaved off their beards.

70
The Greeks liked to look good and admired fit, slim, healthy bodies. Women were praised for their grace and beauty. Young men were admired for their strong figures, and often went without clothes when training for war or taking part in sports competitions. Top athletes became celebrities, and were asked by artists to pose for them as models.

◄ Athletes and their trainer (left) pictured on a Greek vase.

71
Sponges, showers, and swimming helped the Greeks keep clean. Most houses did not have piped water. So people washed themselves by standing under waterfalls, swimming in streams, or squeezing a big sponge full of water over their heads, like a shower.

Gods and goddesses

72 To the Greeks, the world was full of dangers and disasters that they could not understand or control. There were also many good things, such as love, joy, music and beauty, that were wonderful but mysterious. The Greeks thought of all these unknown forces as gods and goddesses who shaped human life and ruled the world.

▶ This statue of the goddess Aphrodite was carved from white marble —a very smooth, delicate stone. It was designed to portray the goddess' perfect beauty. Sadly, it has been badly damaged over the centuries.

▶ Poseidon was god of the sea and storms. He also sent terrifying earthquakes to punish people— or cities—that offended him.

73 Gods and goddesses were pictured as superhuman creatures. They were strong and very beautiful. However, like humans, gods and goddesses also had weaknesses. Aphrodite was thoughtless, Hera was jealous, Apollo and his sister Artemis were cruel, and Ares was bad-tempered.

74 The Greeks believed in magic spirits and monsters. These included Gorgons who turned men to stone, and Sirens—bird-women whose songs lured sailors to their doom. They also believed in witchcraft and curses and tried to fight against them. People painted magic eyes on the prows of their ships to keep a lookout for evil.

▲ Odysseus and his shipmates were surrounded by the Sirens—beautiful half-women, half-bird monsters. They sang sweet songs, calling sailors toward dangerous rocks where their ships were wrecked.

75 Individuals were often anxious to see what the future would bring. They believed that oracles (holy messengers) could see the future. The most famous oracles were at Delphi, where a drugged priestess answered questions, and at Dodona, where the leaves of sacred trees whispered words from the gods.

▶ Herakles was a hero—a man who became a god. He performed amazing feats of strength and fought against many monsters. This statue shows him killing a centaur, half-man, half-horse.

76 Poets and dramatists retold myths and legends about the gods. Some stories were explanations of natural events—thunder was the god Zeus shaking his fist in anger. Others explored bad thoughts and feelings shared by gods and humans, such as greed and disloyalty.

Temples and festivals

77 **In Greece and the lands where the Greeks settled, we can still see the remains of huge, beautiful temples.** They were built as holy homes for gods and goddesses. Each city-state had its own guardian god and many temples housed a huge, lifelike statue of him or her. People hoped that the god's spirit might visit them and live in the statue for a while.

▶ This gigantic statue of the goddess Athena was 50 feet high and was made of gold and ivory. It stood inside her finest temple, the Parthenon in Athens. In her right hand, Athena holds Nike, the goddess of victory.

QUIZ

1. What were temples?
2. Where did all the gods meet?
3. What did people offer to their gods and goddesses?
4. What happened at shrines?

Answers:
1. Holy homes for gods and goddesses 2. Mount Olympus 3. Prayers and sacrifices (gifts) 4. Secret rituals

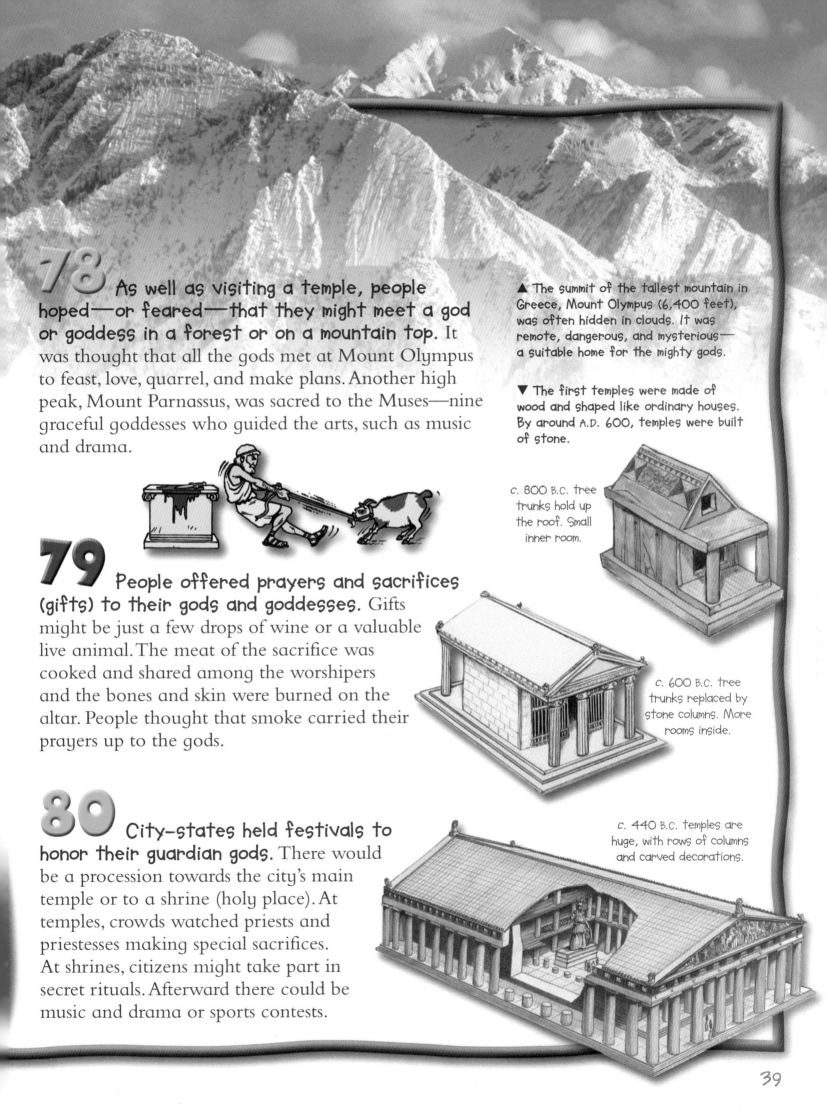

78 As well as visiting a temple, people hoped—or feared—that they might meet a god or goddess in a forest or on a mountain top. It was thought that all the gods met at Mount Olympus to feast, love, quarrel, and make plans. Another high peak, Mount Parnassus, was sacred to the Muses—nine graceful goddesses who guided the arts, such as music and drama.

79 People offered prayers and sacrifices (gifts) to their gods and goddesses. Gifts might be just a few drops of wine or a valuable live animal. The meat of the sacrifice was cooked and shared among the worshipers and the bones and skin were burned on the altar. People thought that smoke carried their prayers up to the gods.

80 City-states held festivals to honor their guardian gods. There would be a procession towards the city's main temple or to a shrine (holy place). At temples, crowds watched priests and priestesses making special sacrifices. At shrines, citizens might take part in secret rituals. Afterward there could be music and drama or sports contests.

▲ The summit of the tallest mountain in Greece, Mount Olympus (6,400 feet), was often hidden in clouds. It was remote, dangerous, and mysterious— a suitable home for the mighty gods.

▼ The first temples were made of wood and shaped like ordinary houses. By around A.D. 600, temples were built of stone.

c. 800 B.C. tree trunks hold up the roof. Small inner room.

c. 600 B.C. tree trunks replaced by stone columns. More rooms inside.

c. 440 B.C. temples are huge, with rows of columns and carved decorations.

39

Olympic Games

81 **The Olympic Games began as a festival to honor Zeus.** Over the centuries, it grew into the greatest sports event in the Greek world. A huge festival complex was built at Olympia with a temple, sports tracks, seats for 40,000 spectators, a campsite and rooms for visitors, and a field full of stalls selling food and drink.

▶ Victory! The Greeks believed that winners were chosen by the gods. The first known Olympic Games was held in 776 B.C., though the festival may have begun years earlier.

82 **Every four years athletes traveled from all over Greece to take part in the Olympic Games.** They had to obey strict rules—respect for Zeus, no fights among competitors, and no weapons anywhere near the sports tracks. In return they claimed protection—the holy Olympic Peace. Anyone who attacked them on their journeys was severely punished.

QUIZ

1. When was the first Olympic Games held?
2. Could women go to the Olympic Games?
3. What did winning athletes wear on their heads?

Answers:
1. 776 B.C., though the festival may have begun years earlier. 2. No. There was a separate women's games held 3. Crowns of holy laurel leaves

40

83 **The most popular events were running, long jump, wrestling, and boxing.** Spectators might also watch chariot races, athletes throwing the discus and javelin, or weightlifting contests. The most prestigious event was the 200-meter sprint. There was also a dangerous fighting contest called *pankration* (total power).

▲ Boxers did not wear gloves. Instead they wrapped their hands in bandages.

84 **Many events featured weapons or skills that were needed in war.** One of the most grueling competitions was a race wearing heavy battle armor. The main Olympic Games were for men only—women could not take part. There was a separate women's games held at Olympia on different years from the men's competitions.

▲ Throwing the discus was a test of strength and balance. It was also useful training for war.

▲ Swimmer Michael Phelps sets a new world record at the Beijing Olympics, 2008. The modern Olympics is modeled on the ancient games and since 1896 has remained the world's greatest sports festival.

85 **Athletes who won Olympic contests were honored as heroes.** They were crowned with wreaths of holy laurel leaves and given valuable prizes of olive oil, fine clothes, and pottery. Poets composed songs in their praise and their home city-states often rewarded them with free food and lodgings for life!

▶ A crown of laurel leaves was given to winning athletes as a sign of their godlike strength and speed.

Plays and poems

86 Greek drama originated at religious festivals. In the earliest rituals, priests and priestesses sometimes played the part of gods or goddesses. They acted out stories told about them or famous local heroes. Over the years, these ancient rituals changed into a new art form—drama.

87 Drama became so popular that many city-states built splendid new open-air theaters. Greek theaters were built in a half-circle shape with tiers (raised rows) of seats looking down over an open space for performers. Most seats were filled by men—women were banned from many plays.

▶ The theater at Epidaurus, in southern Greece, is one of the largest built by the ancient Greeks. It had seats for over 10,000 spectators.

88 **All the parts in a play were performed by men.** They wore masks, wigs, and elaborate costumes to look like women or magic spirits and monsters. Some theaters had ladders and cranes so that actors playing gods could appear to fly or sit among the clouds.

89 **In some city-states, especially Athens, drama remained an important part of several religious festivals.** Writers competed for prizes for the best new plays. They wrote serious plays called tragedies, and lively comedies. Some plays lasted all day long. Others had extra "satyr plays" added on. These were short, funny pieces.

▶ Actors wore masks to show which character they were playing. Bright-colored masks were for cheerful characters and dark-colored masks were more gloomy. Some masks were double-sided so that the actors could change parts quickly.

90 **Plays were written like poetry.** The main actors were always accompanied by singers and dancers. Poems were also recited to music. Tunes were sad for tragic poems or rousing for those about war. Poets performed at men's dinner parties and in rich families' homes. Public storytellers entertained crowds by singing poems in the streets.

Barbarian—or monster—with wild, shaggy hair

Angry young man

Huge, funnel-shaped mouths helped the actors' words reach the audience

Masks with beards and bald heads were for actors playing old men

Scientists and thinkers

91 **The Greeks liked to ask questions and discuss.** Although they believed in gods and magic, they also wanted to investigate the world in a practical way. They learned some mathematics and astronomy from the Egyptians and Babylonians then used this knowledge to find out more for themselves.

▶ Hipparchus (170–126 B.C.) observed and recorded the position of over 800 stars and worked out a way of measuring their brightness.

92 **Mathematicians and astronomers made important discoveries.** Aristarchus was the first to understand that the Earth travels around the Sun. Hipparchus mapped the stars. Thales discovered mathematical laws about circles and triangles. Pythagoras worked out the mathematics behind music and measured the movements of the Sun and the Moon.

93 **Many people believed that illness was a punishment sent by the gods.** However doctors, led by Hippocrates (460–370 B.C.), tried to cure people with good food, fresh air, exercise, and herbal medicines. They carefully observed patients for signs of illness and recorded the results of their prescriptions. That way they could prove scientifically which treatments worked best for each disease.

▲ This stone carving shows a doctor treating an injured arm. Greek doctors were some of the first in the world to treat patients scientifically.

▼ Archimedes was the most famous Greek engineer. He invented (or improved) a spiral pump to make water flow uphill, for example, from rivers into fields.

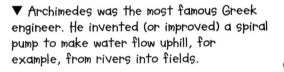
Handle turns wooden screw

Water is lifted round and round and then pushed out

Water is pulled in as the screw turns

94 **Engineers designed many clever machines.** Speakers at the Athenian Assembly were timed by a water-powered clock and there were machines that used hot air to open temple doors. Archimedes (287–211 B.C.) discovered how objects float and how they balance. He also designed a "sun gun" (huge glass lens) to focus the Sun's rays on enemy ships to set them on fire.

95 **Greek thinkers thought about thinking!** As well as investigating the world and creating new inventions they also wanted to understand people and society. Questions such as "How do we think?", "How do we see and feel?", and "How can we live the best lives?" were important to them.

Ancient Greek heritage

96 **The ancient Greeks lived over 2,000 years ago, but still influence our lives today.** Many people still admire the democratic system of government that Greek city-states invented. The Olympic Games, revived in 1896, is still the greatest sporting contest in the world. And today's plays, films, musicals, and TV series have their origins, long ago, in Greek religious drama.

▼ A Greek temple on Sicily. Its massive ruins still impress visitors today.

97 **Many modern words and names have developed from ancient Greek originals.** Greek-inspired words include "telephone," "television," and "music." Greek personal names, such as Chloe, Penelope, Jason, and Philip, are still popular today. Many places around the Mediterranean have names that reveal their Greek origins—Naples, in Italy, was Neapolis (New City) to the Greeks.

98 **Today's ways of writing are copied from the ancient Greeks.** The Greek alphabet was invented around 1000–800 B.C., after scribes in Phoenicia (now Lebanon) became the first to use written signs (letters) to represent separate sounds. The Greeks made good use of that amazing idea and passed their alphabet on to the Romans. From there, it spread throughout Europe—and then all round the world.

▲ In Washington D.C., the White House (home of the President of the U.S.A.) has design features borrowed from Greek buildings, such as the porch with tall columns.

100 Traces of ancient Greek civilization still survive. When Greece was conquered by invaders, many important writings and works of art were lost and buildings were destroyed. Some survived because they were copied by the Romans. Greek culture was rediscovered by European thinkers around A.D. 1400–1600 and inspired artists for centuries. Today, the ruins of great Greek buildings still survive. Poems and plays are still read and acted, and many works of art are preserved in museums.

99 We copy Greek designs for clothes and buildings. Fashion designers dress models and filmstars in styles copied from Greek clothes. For hundreds of years, impressive buildings have included Greek design features, such as tall, fluted (ridged) columns. Even very modern buildings make use of Greek ideas about proportion (shape and size).

▼ Repairing the Parthenon, Athens, 2004. Ancient Greek buildings are national treasures that make citizens and governments feel proud.

Index